Jesus *for* Kids
Teaching *Dance* and Sharing *Faith*

An essential manual to ignite your dance teaching journey, full of practical ways to teach, deliver and shape workshops alongside your Christian faith.

ANNA GILDERSON

Autumn Pearl Publishing

Copyright © 2021 Anna Gilderson

All rights reserved. No part of this book may be reproduced or used in any manner without the prior written permission of the copyright owner, except for the use of brief quotations in a book review.

ISBN 978-1-7398401-0-5
eBook ISBN 978-1-7398401-1-2

Book cover and layout by Spurwing Creative

Scripture quotations taken from The Holy Bible, New International Version® NIV®
Copyright © 1973 1978 1984 2011 by Biblica, Inc.™
Used by permission. All rights reserved worldwide.

'It's a New Day' song lyrics, used with permission.
Copyright © 2016 Dan Adams and Gareth Loh.

Autumn Pearl Publishing

Contents

Introduction   1

Part One – Building a Strong Foundation

1. My story   8
2. Scriptures that tell a story   16

Part Two – Commit to the Journey

3. Why dance?   28
4. Why faith?   34
5. Why children?   40

Part Three – Equipping a Generation

6. Just remember   50
7. Getting started   56
8. Winning workshop structure   60
9. Confidence in leading children   70
10. Creative prayer, children and dancing   76

Part Four – Moving Forward

11. Ready-to-go workshops   86
    - Jonah and the whale   88
    - Go, go, go Joseph   91
    - Family Advent fun   94
    - The Lord is my shepherd   97
    - The faith of a mustard seed   99

Glossary of Terms   103

Resources   105

Other Movement Ideas – Games and Action Songs   106

About the Author   109

About UC Grace   111

INTRODUCTION

When was the last time you felt joy? Pure, indescribable joy? Can you pinpoint it? Children ooze joy; they display it with all the colours of the rainbow. Whether life is good or bad, they love sharing the excitement that joy brings. Children love to dance and they love it when you dance with them.

But it can be daunting, can't it? Stepping out and dancing with children or even teaching children. Finding a starting point, a theme, knowing how to include your faith with what you are teaching – there is so much to think about!

This book is here to provide you with knowledge so you can radiate joy and excitement as you step out to teach children dance and movement with the Christian faith.

You will find in here:

- Strategies to develop your own teaching style.
- Scripture relevant to children, dance and your journey.
- Ready-to-go lesson plans.
- Teaching and planning techniques.

Plus, so many other useful bits of information that will help you feel more confident when you step out in front of children.

I've written this book out of a passion to share with others my joy for teaching children. It's so important that we invest our time in them and allow them the opportunity to grow, explore and develop in a safe space.

With the right tools, they have the chance to develop into amazing, strong people, full of joy about life and recognising the excitement that Jesus, dancing and movement can bring.

So grab a notebook and be ready to answer questions and put things into action as you begin this journey to ignite your teaching.

How to get the most from this book

At regular intervals in the book you will find an 'activity' box. These are designed to help you implement what you have just read. This may involve reflection on your journey of faith, planning an aspect of a workshop or deciding elements of your practice that are important to you.

If you take the time to work through the questions and suggestions, you will discover new ideas, teaching techniques and connect your faith to dance and movement in a stronger way. Your teaching practice and skills can only grow as you make the choice to not just read but implement what you read.

I'll be praying that God stirs your heart throughout your time reading this book. May you have the confidence to let God lead in the moments that you struggle and trust that his goodness will shine through all the time. God has already placed inside you the skills that you need to teach and lead.

Give him the space to work alongside you and learn together!

Part One
Building a Strong Foundation

Part One: Building a Strong Foundation

"As you grow in dance, you grow in God. As you grow in God, you expand your dance."

-1-
MY STORY

My memories

> *I'm standing at the corner, behind the other children, waiting for my turn to travel across the room. We're doing gallops today. A little excited bubble grew up inside me. I LOVE gallops, that ability to cross the space swiftly and effectively; I feel such a sense of freedom.*

~

> *The song that brings me joy begins to be played by the worship band. I'm hopping about at the back because I know what my reaction will be. The pulse in my heart calls me to move and dance with the other children down the aisle, splitting off in different ways as we arrive at the front.*
>
> *We've each got a flag in our hand; mine's silver, always silver for God's glory and because I love it. Encouraging us is Barry. Barry always had so much energy and worshipped with an openness I was desperate for. His only focus was Jesus. I wanted that – to worship where nothing gets in the way. Where my heart displayed the pure delight for following Jesus.*
>
> *Even now 'Days of Elijah' causes my feet to start tapping, a smile on my face and the itchiness to get my body moving and praising Jesus.*

Welcome to some of my most vibrant memories of dancing for God as a child – the freedom and release as a child dancing for God, plus the freedom and release that movement gave me as I galloped, all experienced whilst at Guildford Baptist Church and watching, learning and witnessing alongside others.

Both of these experiences brought me to an early understanding that dance and movement impacted my heart in a way that I didn't understand.

It always seemed particularly touched when I danced in worship, but I couldn't correlate it to my faith at the time.

I do know that because someone invested time, energy and patience in me, I had a love of seeking God's presence instilled in me from a young age. I had someone that not only demonstrated how movement could be used but exuded the desire to lavish that on others, simply through the act of sharing. It was infectious.

By someone taking the time to 'be' all they could be in worship and before God, they created a role model for me and others to follow.

Dancing down the aisles to 'Days of Elijah' is still such a vivid memory of my first time using flags. I recognised the power of simple movements and a desire to seek more. The close-knit family that formed out of my early years at church provided a safe space to explore; it was nurturing, encouraging and fun! All these things are important for a child to flourish.

Now my own faith journey has had its twists and turns. Often, if you grow up in a Christian family it can be hard to pinpoint when (you say) you gave your life to Jesus; everything seems to roll into one and you move from one thing to the next, perhaps without taking a pause. I consider it to be the moment you choose to live your faith actively. Taking ownership of your beliefs and actions and turning to God as the person to lead and guide you.

It was 2000 when I made that decision. I chose that active step. What was the impetus? Why then?

Put simply, a movement signal! The simple act of walking under a flag of fire and a flag of water was like a trigger. Wow! A *simple* action created *profound* results, including an immediate burning desire to get close to God through movement. From that point, movement was part of my worship; it was my whole heart. I didn't understand what happened when I did it, but I knew something shifted. The status and pull of my heart detected that.

In the years following that point, I had the privilege to lead summer events with Powerpack Children's Ministries. During that time I was able to witness and experience the power of the Holy Spirit in children.

It was here that I was encouraged (and given the opportunity) to lead dance worship academies, beginning my teaching journey to share my love of dance and movement with faith.

People told me they were blessed when I danced. I didn't understand that. To me, I was just dancing for Jesus. But then I started pausing when I was teaching children in those very first years (2000–2006) and began to recognise a move in the Spirit as they danced, and I started to get it. I began to really understand that it all starts with the heart, but it also all starts with the children. They are the ones that will pass on to others what they are taught, what they see and what they learn. We have the ability to demonstrate, teach and share how they can go deeper with Jesus using their dance and movement, so why don't we make that a priority?

In the years since that early recognition of seeing the Holy Spirit interact through dance and movement, a passion had grown to keep teaching, to keep sharing and to put our children, even the very little ones, at the forefront of the need to share how creativity, individuality and the Holy Spirit should be front and centre in their lives. I love sharing this phrase of mine:

"As you grow in dance, you grow in God. As you grow in God, you expand your dance."

It is all connected and it moves in a circle. Each one affecting the other. Part of that cycle is practising responding to the Holy Spirit and honing in to recognising when the Holy Spirit gives a nudge. This has taken me time but has made me more aware of my journey and conversation with God. These things were key:

- Talking to God and then allowing time to listen.
- Realising that the reasons you move may be different to what others interpret in your movement.
- Acknowledging where you have the chance to be blessed and bless others.
- To look for the *grace* in that moment and seize that conversation with God.

My teaching

As I went deeper with these things, my desire to share my experiences and learning with others moved up my chain of priority. After all, the depth of our faith helps us display who God has made us be, the unique qualities and purpose He's written into our lives.

In Joshua 1:3, we learn how God knows each place our foot will tread. So He knows what you need to teach dance, movement and about Him. All the steps are before you; it's how you choose to tread them.

Over time, as my teaching practice grew, I discovered certain things underpinned my delivery and interaction. Heart being a major one. Our hearts influence much of what we do. The journey of UC Grace wouldn't be where it is now without the influence of my heart. However, who am I doing this for? God. Therefore, God's heart needs to shine through stronger than mine.

> *Create in me a pure heart, O God, and renew a steadfast spirit within me*
> *(Psalm 51:10).*

What does it look like when I combine God's heart for me and others and my heart for God and others?

The result is the opportunity to:

- Provide a safe space for people to deepen their knowledge of who they are in God.
- Realise the depth of love God has for them no matter what.
- Lay at His cross those things which they are struggling with.
- Lean with their whole bodyweight onto God in complete trust.

In other words, God's heart steadies my soul.

Seeking God's heart renews the spirit within me to keep putting him first in all I do and to keep 'creating' moments where the impact of a movement language equips participants (in the case of this book, children). Giving space for God's heart takes the participant deeper into God's word and the ability for them to decide themselves the path they want to take.

You can't share your heart without passion…

When you worship, you are choosing to share in something that is powerful and special to you. Worship will mean different things to different people, and how you interact with worship can be different to someone else.

Worship is a place your passion can be displayed. I have this phrase, 'passion in a suitcase'. For quite a while, my circumstances meant I had to move around, living in different places, adapting and changing how both UC Grace ran, as well as 're-starting' my life due to military postings with my husband. Each time my passion was not lost but put into a suitcase. How I unpacked it when I arrived at my new destination always depended on God.

The season you are in will determine how your passion influences your worship. How we let God lead and guide us through that moment can carry us through those moments when we need to both receive and demonstrate grace.

How does your passion influence your worship?

The combination of God's heart and passion provides me with a purpose to use dance to communicate with God. It encourages me to sink my roots deep into the solid foundation that comes from the Bible, using this as the impetus to create a movement language.

Part of those roots is the 'armour of God'. This is an amazing symbol of the 'equipment' that God gives us to worship and follow him. By choosing to raise our arms whilst singing in praise and worship, kneel in response to the words of a song or bow our heads to pray, we are creating movement and putting purpose into our journey.

Using the word 'dancer' might be too strong for you. Instead, consider a phrase my husband likes to use: 'I don't dance; I move well'. For him, having the association of being a dancer is too strong, but he will happily say that he moves well and enjoys doing so when he does. Perhaps for you, this is the preferred way of looking at it: moving well and moving with God.

God gives us freedom to demonstrate our journey the way we need to. He also gives us the Holy Spirit, to enable us to grasp a deeper understanding of walking with Jesus.

> *It is for freedom that Christ has set us free*
> *(Galatians 5:1).*

Faith and dance stimulate a different perspective on our relationship with God. As we step out to dance, our language of movement grows, igniting a flame within us. The image of a flame is often representative of the Holy Spirit. Even the smallest embers of a fire still have a glow, a flame that can be fanned. How much excitement do you feel when you see a big fire? There's the feeling of ecstasy, fun, relaxation, happiness, freedom and more all rolled into one.

> *But the Advocate, the Holy Spirit, whom the Father will send in my name, will teach you all things and will remind you of everything I have said to you*
> *(John 14:26).*

ACTIVITY

A simple exercise you can try is to think about 'passing on the fire inside'. Think about a ball of light that is inside you, wanting to grow – a tiny little flame. Flames are not always big to start with – they grow. As you imagine this flame glowing and growing inside you, how does it encourage you to start moving your body in reaction to this?

The Holy Spirit is always inside us. Sometimes it is a still, small flame, other times a raging fire. We need to have the courage to let the fire grow and move in our lives as God would want it.

What is your movement and dance journey?

In your notebook, write down your own personal journey with dance, movement and worship. Do you have any favourite memories? Did someone or something specific inspire you? Has there been an impact on your heart and attitude to God?

-2-
SCRIPTURES THAT TELL A STORY...

> *Therefore, everyone who hears these words of mine and puts them into practice is like a wise man who built his house on the rock*
> *(Matthew 7:24).*

Wow! The Bible is the best book to read! It's full of ways of living life to the fullest, ways to seek support and encouragement in times of despair. Not to mention how its words can ground us, crown us and declare our individuality. It's a great tool for you to use for growing your teaching ministry.

The above verse from Matthew cheers us on to keep grounded in God's word as we move through life. It is for this reason that teaching about God's word is essential during your children's workshops. Let me elaborate by looking at the following areas:

1. Scripture as the foundation for workshops
2. Scripture in relation to movement

Both of these areas interchange with each other. Moving forward with your teaching ministry, it is helpful for you to recognise what you are leaning your knowledge, heart and faith on, and why.

Scripture as the foundation for workshops

Part of giving our lives to follow Jesus involves reading and grounding ourselves in His word. Think of it as an unending cycle:

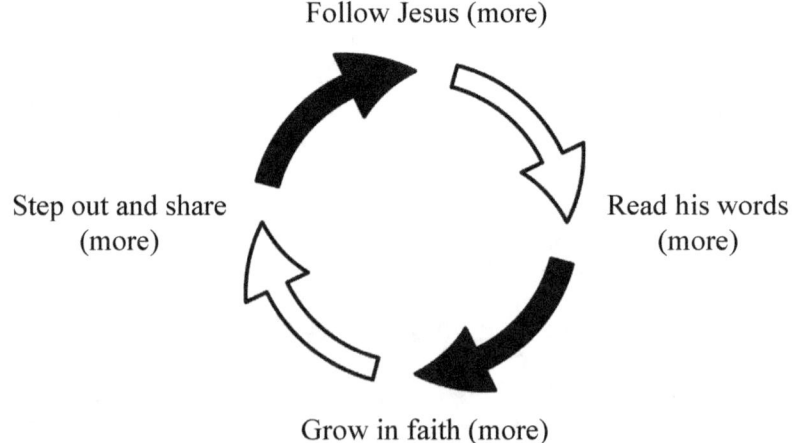

Understanding the reasons why you run a worship dance workshop (whether for children or adults) is important. But more than that is recognising the cycle above.

This cycle of learning, growing and stepping out with God's word should form an essential part of any workshop that you deliver. Whether you use it as a focus at the beginning or reflection at the end, or even something that grows and goes deeper during the whole workshop. You are creating an impact with God's word by putting it front and centre of what you are doing and asking God to lead and guide you as you move.

Children have the innate ability to remember things in ways adults can't, mostly by association. I am a massive fan of teaching children by association (more on that later). It helps to embed in their memory and encourages their recapping skills. Using Scripture as the foundation for a children's workshop is fun! Here are just a few ways that you can get children moving and remembering Scripture:

1. Find the Scripture – hide various pieces of the Scripture around the room. Each time they 'discover' a piece of the Scripture, associate a movement with it.

2. Simon says (except it's Jesus says) – pick sections of the Scripture and repeat it in different ways, with or without an action. You could also think about the tone and level of your voice. Does that change how the children react to the Scripture?

3. Get the children involved – break down the Scripture and encourage the children to think of movements for different parts of the Scripture, taking the time to talk about the words that they pick out and what they mean.

You will learn about it later in the book, but repetition and demonstration is so important when putting Scripture in front of children (and adults).

The more you do, the more natural it is for them and you, and it will soon come to be an expected part of the routine when you deliver a workshop. So do not be afraid to put God's word front and centre; we learn so much from it!

Scripture in relation to movement

When it comes to using Scripture with dance and movement, the Bible is one big playground. So much to play and learn. Let's meet some verses that introduce us to dance in Scripture and how we could interpret them.

Let's begin in Exodus. God has just brought the Israelites to safety, out of Egypt through the Red Sea.

> *Then Miriam the prophet, Aaron's sister, took a timbrel in her hand, and all the women followed her, with timbrels and dancing*
> *(Exodus 15:20).*

Despite the bad situation they may be in, Miriam chooses to do a praise dance for victory – victory on escaping out of Egypt, for God saving them. Not to mention declaring heartfelt thanks to God for His help. Often, as humans, we focus on the negative and whizz past the positive. This verse encourages us that praising God in all circumstances, big or small, is important.

The story of David in some form is known well. We pick up the story in 2 Samuel 6:14–16.

> *Wearing a linen ephod, David was dancing before the* Lord *with all his might, while he and all Israel were bringing up the ark of the* Lord *with shouts and the sound of trumpets.*
>
> *As the ark of the* Lord *was entering the City of David, Michal daughter of Saul watched from a window. And when she saw King David leaping and dancing before the* Lord, *she despised him in her heart.*

This sets the context of David dancing. First, we read that he danced with all his might. Imagine doing something with every ounce of energy that you have. We then read that someone who saw David dancing despised what she saw. How would you feel if you completed something with all your energy but received a negative response?

The passage continues with further detail about how David danced and David's response to this challenge.

> *When David returned home to bless his household, Michal daughter of Saul came out to meet him and said, "How the king of Israel has distinguished himself today, going around half-naked in full view of the slave girls of his servants as any vulgar fellow would!"*
>
> *David said to Michal, "It was before the LORD, who chose me rather than your father or anyone from his house when he appointed me ruler over the LORD's people Israel—I will celebrate before the LORD. I will become even more undignified than this, and I will be humiliated in my own eyes. But by these slave girls you spoke of, I will be held in honor"*
>
> *(2 Samuel 6:20–22).*

His only priority, as he worshipped, was God, not what others thought of him. Don't let your fear of what others think stop you from stepping out to worship God. David chose to put God first. To be thankful for the situation and only focus on God through it. What instances in your life can you recall when you have made a choice to do this too?

In the two examples we have looked at so far, dance has played a role in the communication of feelings, emotions and situations. This continues in Psalm 30:11.

> *You turned my wailing into dancing; you removed my sackcloth and clothed me with joy.*

Dancing through our emotions helps us to process the tough times. It might not solve it, but choosing to thank and trust God in those situations helps us in our journey. This is shown too in Luke 15:25.

> *"Meanwhile, the older son was in the field. When he came near the house, he heard music and dancing.*

How often do we rejoice when we find something that has been lost? What emotions do you go through? Relief? Sadness? Pure joy? We all react differently.

God is calling us to celebrate! To notice the return. In the parable, the celebration here is that, although the son may have left with everything, he chose to come back with nothing and simply serve. However, his father just wanted to celebrate he was home. When we make that choice to follow Jesus, share him, serve him or be with him, Jesus has a massive celebration. As we read in so many verses, our journey to follow Jesus requires our whole being – not part, but all.

In Acts 17:28 we hear:

> *'For in him we live and move and have our being.' As some of your own poets have said, 'We are his offspring.'*

God is calling us in the verse to inhabit him. To make following him naturally part of our everyday life – living, breathing and being. It's also one of my favourite verses that gives us a call to move. In Genesis, God breathed life into us (Genesis 2:7), He created us and then moved us.

This Scripture in Acts offers us not only a reminder of what God did but an encouragement to be a child and to see God as a parent.

ACTIVITY

Wherever you are in your dance and movement journey, this is a great verse to meditate on. Consider three clear things the verse mentions:

1. Living
2. Moving
3. Being

How are you living your faith at the moment? What movements are already woven into your journey? Start by imagining God breathing life into you and giving you 'being'. What sort of reaction happens within your body?

Remember how I said the Bible was a big playground?

There are many more verses that talk about movement – positive and negative. Why not take some time to explore the Bible and see what other verses you can find. How could you use it, learn from it and take it on your journey of faith?

ACTION

Which verse encourages you in your worship?

Each of us will have verses that speak to us in different ways. What are your favourite ones? Is there just one that you can focus on as you go further through this book? It can act as an encourager and acknowledgement that God is with you on this journey.

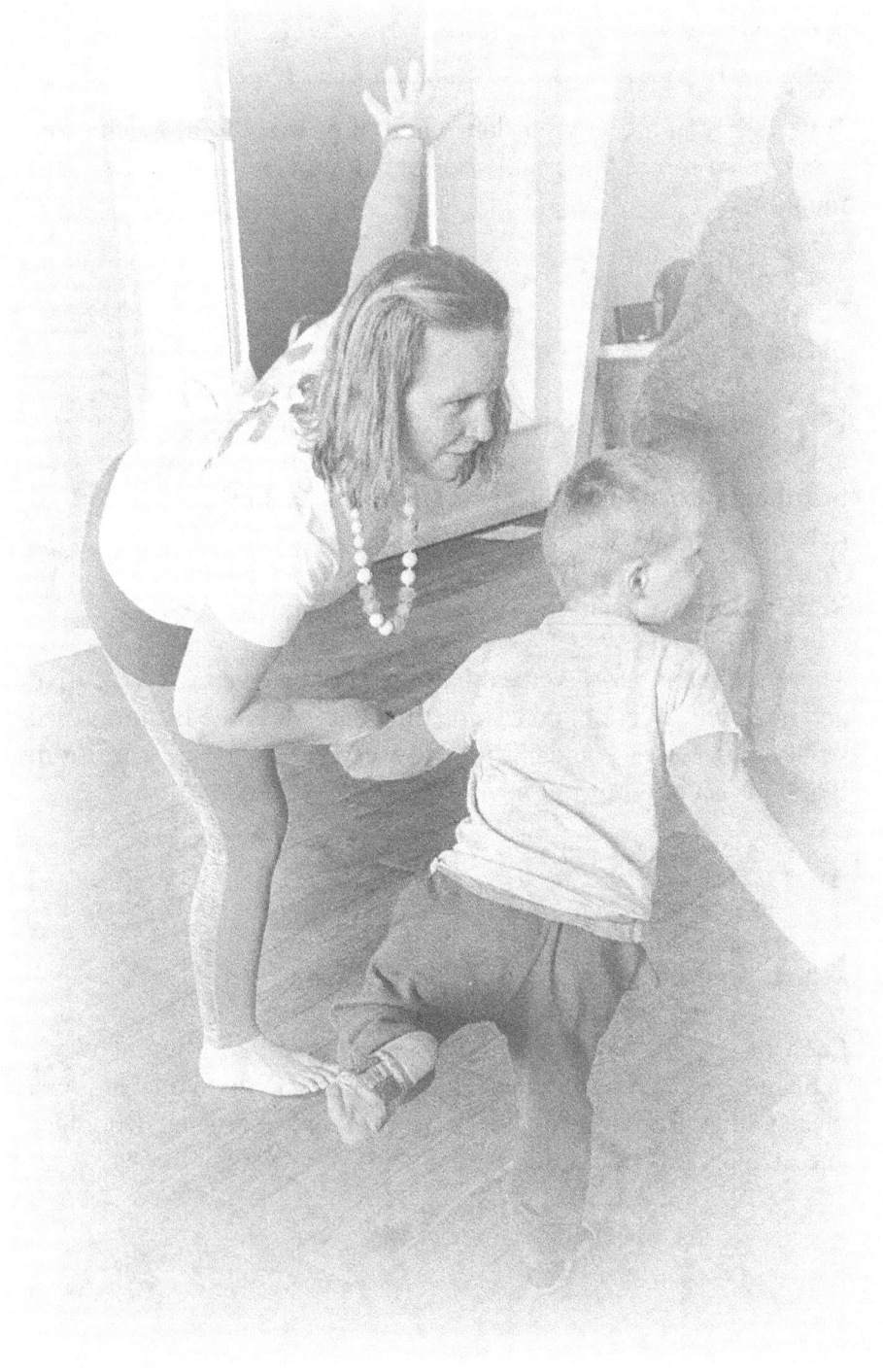

Part Two

Commit to the Journey

Part Two: Commit to the Journey

"If you model having a conversation with God, they will see how natural and normal that can be."

-3-
WHY DANCE?

Observations

Dance brings a freedom and release that is unparalleled in any other physical activity. The emotions it invokes and the thoughts it brings allow both the mover and observer to experience two quite different things.

Over the many years dance has been part of my life, I have seen its ability to cross boundaries, cultures and religions. It allows the unspoken to be spoken and the unseen to be seen in multiple ways. The very essence of dance is mystery, journey, intrigue and depth all at the same time.

Often, you can never attach the same single word to consistently describe a dance you see. Each time you see it, different things will sparkle. Different movements, expressions, accents in the music and emotions from the dancers will grab your attention.

When I dance, it's like I enter a whole different world. A peek into the rawness of my heart and what it's experiencing in that moment. Movement becomes my language when there are no words to say – my exercise I can get lost in and my peace I can inhale. This movement language beats to the rhythm of my heart. If my heart is sluggish and slow, my dance will show that; if it's full of joy and energy, it will show that.

What I express and feel will be different to what others see and feel. That is the beauty of dance. It's what makes it hard to create a true record – there is not always an outcome that is visible to all who see and take part. With Christian dance, the outcome often equates to changes in mental state and a deeper understanding of Jesus.

An example of this is when I watch my daughter dance, freely, with no obvious agenda that I can see. Yet, what I observe as she moves her hands in a delicate and prescribed way, is she knows exactly where that movement is going and what it makes her feel as she does it.

As the observer, I see a girl lost in movement. I see excitement, I see passion and I also see tenderness. I feel joy as I watch her move and it lifts my spirits when they need it. But what my daughter is experiencing as she dances is freedom and the chance to calm down.

What are your experiences of observing dance? What you see or create is individual to you. This includes the impact on your heart, journey of faith and feelings.

Movements

My observations of dance have blown me away. It's an uninhibited yet vulnerable form of exploration. Helen Poynor[1] expresses how if we "accept that anybody is potentially a dancing body... any movement has the potential to be a dance movement". What worship looks like for one, won't be the same for another. The result of this means our interaction with worship is different for everyone. Movement and dance are one of the ways you can interact with worship. Worship is part of our everyday life. The movements that we make, however small, can form part of our worship to God.

The biggest hill is often accepting that you are a dancer even if you move just a little, like I mentioned in Chapter 1.

Different styles of dance demonstrate emotions and stories in different ways. As you worship you may realise that you don't sit in one 'style'. Instead you create your own style that draws upon your various learnings. Dance for me isn't about working within a prescribed syllabus or style but exploring, growing and developing a movement language that is my own.

Since UC Grace began, I have had the privilege of meeting/teaching many dancers who started with me in 2010 and are still dancing with me now. The movement language they had when they first began their dance and movement journey with me is completely different to their movement language now. This can be attributed to many reasons, including how they respond to their journey with God, dancing alongside others and investing in time to develop their passion, as well as acknowledging the progress they have made and always seeking to put Jesus at the centre of their movements.

---

[1] Amans, D. (2008) *An Introduction to Community Dance Practice*, Palgrave Macmillan, p. 88.

Where you choose to put God in the relationship of movement, dance and faith will not only determine the richness of growth within your movement language but also the recognition of how much movement can encompass your *whole* day. Part of this is how both everyday and specific movements can integrate together, growing your movement and prayer life.

Case study – Beth

I want to talk about one lady called Beth[2]. I first met Beth in 2011, when she attended one of my first Living Colour sessions. Living Colour workshops are all about providing a chance for people to explore Christian dance safely through different exercises.

Beth wanted to see how dance could be used more in worship. As she journeyed, exploring flags, developing dance techniques, growing in confidence and trying other ways of moving, Beth recognised that using worship dance was just the beginning. Through the safety of the workshops, Beth experienced how dance could take you through your deepest despairs and instil a physical knowledge that God was with you through all things.

Ten years on, Beth has been able to explore dance styles and, using what she has learnt, has developed her own style. As I watched her dance recently, I could see how God has taken her dance on its own journey from one place to another. Watching the progression of this journey has been a privilege.

I love dance so much because what it demonstrates is beyond what can be written succinctly. The whole journey is down to the experience both as a viewer *and* a participant (more on this in Chapter 5). Since Beth developed her movement language and the depth of her relationship to God, her life has seen such a richness of growth which she can now use as she steps out to teach and share with others that same passion I shared with her.

---

[2] Name has been changed.

ACTIVITY

Why do you dance?

Think of some of the times that you have danced – church, parties, weddings, kitchen, home – any place that you have had a wiggle. In those moments that you dance and move, why is it that you do it? Think about your physical state, your heart and your emotions.

-4-
WHY FAITH?

Faith is something that is personal to an individual. Everyone will have some form of faith, whether they choose it to be in God or in something else.

Hope often gets associated with faith. The word 'hope' inspires a positive way forward, invoking a sense of something far greater to come, whilst faith can help you understand, deal with the situation and move on with it with focus and stability.

Faith helps to instil a firm foundation; a firm foundation requires grounding, something to keep us connected to the floor but helps us move through life. In Christianity, that grounding is Jesus.

> *Therefore everyone who hears these words of mine and puts them into practice is like a wise man who built his house on the rock (Matthew 7:24).*

We first read this verse at the beginning of Chapter 2. I'm sharing it here again as it serves as a great reminder of our journey of faith. As a Christian, I choose to hear God's word and put my faith in Jesus. Knowing that he died and rose again, taking away my sins. I know He walks with me as I do life, and I believe His word, the Bible, is something greater that requires trust, dedication and passion to understand it to its fullest potential.

Let me give you a bit more insight into my journey of faith.

For those Christians that have been brought up in Christian homes, there is often a turning point that allows them to identify that they chose to make the faith their own.

By that I mean, they have grown up with the practices, beliefs and understanding of a Christian faith but hadn't chosen to acknowledge and own it for themselves, until that point.

This very clearly happened to me as a teenager when I was flung into leading with a ministry called Powerpack Children's Ministries. I say flung because it was literally in-at-the-deep-end, Holy Spirit whispering stuff. It was here that I recognised this thing about having a faith and believing in Jesus really was real. My dancing shoes were quite literally put on. I experienced that inexplicable pull of God signalling to my heart that I needed to dance. I needed to respond to this big pull. This feeling or signal was what I needed to learn more about, to discern, develop and respond.

Since that point, I have always been very aware of the need to have God at the centre of what I do. The reality of this as a teenager was hard.

Faith is something that will stand the test of time; it will adapt and mould as circumstances and situations arise. What's important is what is underneath the faith holding it in place – your foundation or roots!

In varying circumstances, since that realisation that I had to own my faith, I have had to sink my roots into God, allowing God's word to be my strength and my foundation.

One of my earliest memories of this was in 2004 when my youth leader died very suddenly. This was a man who demonstrated how to be passionate for Jesus, putting him first in all circumstances. He encouraged me in my dancing, planting seeds of what God could and would do. Most of all, I saw first-hand how someone lived their life when there were none but Jesus. After his death, I had a lot of anger. Had I not seen how he leant into God when things got tough, I wouldn't have realised that was possible. Thankfully, as I worked through the anger, I had others surround me with love, God's word and the encouragement that leaning on God in the tough times is part of faith, making the choice to turn to God in all circumstances.

> *So then, just as you received Christ Jesus as Lord, continue to live your lives in him, rooted and built up in him, strengthened in the faith as you were taught, and overflowing with thankfulness.*
>
> *See to it that no one takes you captive through hollow and deceptive philosophy, which depends on human tradition and the elemental spiritual forces of this world rather than on Christ*
>
> *(Colossians 2:6–8).*

Fast forward a couple of decades and those moments to lean on God when the going gets tough are still coming. God has given us a choice, a choice to believe and follow him. That's why we have free will.

ACTIVITY

Faith is such a hard word to unpack. It really is personal to you. But why faith and movement? Because the Bible says so! Simply glance back at Chapter 2 if you need a little refresher.

Why do you have faith?

Think about your journey to becoming a Christian. What encouraged you to make that step? What still encourages you now to maintain your faith?

-5-
WHY CHILDREN?

> *Jesus said, "Let the little children come to me and do not hinder them, for the kingdom of heaven belongs to such as these (Matthew 19:14).*

Whatever way you look at it, children are the next generation. As I like to say, they are the ones who will 'be testimony to the great events', enabling forward movement from the past and striving to implement the great events to come.

For this reason we should offer children the chance to build their future. If they are the ones building it, surely we want to ensure that they are equipped with all the right things to live life and lead well.

Children have the innate ability to get up and do, to charge about life not absorbed in the chain reaction of the whirlwind that may happen as they move on. They see life and they live it.

The ability to express emotions and life is the biggest arsenal that children have. If they want or need to scream, run, jump, laugh or be different, then they will. Their emotions lead them.

God encourages us to be childlike with our faith. But what does 'childlike' mean to you?

I see it as someone who is carefree, who knows their wants and needs and embraces change. They are also looking for opportunities, moving, running and stepping out into a life they are choosing to make their own. This is very much how many children live their life.

Watching children grow, develop and experience new things brings delight into my life. If God calls us to come to Him as a child, let us do that to experience the delight.

Why dance, faith and children?

Each of these things – dance, faith and children, bring a lot of impact as individual elements, but can be brought together to make a whole and the atmosphere shifts.

- **Dance** brings the opportunity for dancer and observer to experience an ever-evolving journey.

- **Faith** allows that evolving journey to create a connection between dancer, observer and God.

- **Children** collide dance and faith together and demonstrate the freedom that God has given us as we go through life.

Drawing these three elements together, we can recognise an innocence in the movement language children bring. This includes the connection between hearing God's word and moving. Children respond without overthinking, displaying their heart and enjoying the chance to have fun getting to know God.

Remember the cycle diagram in Chapter 2? Each part of the cycle impacts the one preceding and the one after. Consider it like a conversation or getting to know God.

Chatting with God is just like having a conversation between you and me. We give the time to share, take the time to listen and then acknowledge anything or action anything that needs doing.

Kids get this. They want this. They are at a prime time to share as they eagerly jump into making friends and simply chatting and sharing life. They are impressionable; that is noticeably clear, as they have no one else to model life from, apart from those that they see around them.

If you model having a conversation with God, they will see how natural and normal that can be. In equal measure, if you demonstrate how you draw close to God through your movement language, children get it! Thus, the connection of dancer, observer and God combine.

Dance can model grace and freedom, where children can be as creative as they want to be. They can hone their understanding of their faith as they move, in the safety of a space where their journey is as important as the movement.

A great example of how this could be is the Lord's Prayer. A tool God has given us to pray deeper and learn more about Him. In 2017, I was part of a Thy Kingdom Come event at Guildford Cathedral. I drew together a team of seven dancers to perform. One thing that we performed was the Lord's Prayer – putting movement to Scripture and then expanding that through dance and movement. At one of the rehearsals, there was one lady with her little boy. He was 2 years old and had watched only a snapshot of another rehearsal, but as his mum stood up to speak and move to the Lord's Prayer, he joined in, copying the movements and picking out the words he could say.

This is what it's all about. It's about God's word being a natural part of our children's lives. It's about providing them with opportunities to explore it in a way that isn't sitting on their bottoms, encouraging a healthy way for them to develop a personal relationship with Jesus.

ACTIVITY

Why do you want to share with children?

Reading this book indicates some desire to better understand the workings of teaching children. But take some time to really think about why you want to share with children.

Is there a memory from your childhood? Did someone leave a lasting influence on your life? Do you just delight in enabling, growing and providing opportunities for children?

Whatever your answer is, spend some time with God, talking to him about your answer to this question. Make a note of anything He shares back with you about how He has created you and the skills and talents He has put inside you.

Part Three
Equipping a Generation

"As a teacher you have the opportunity to *demonstrate, inspire* and be a *role model* to the youngest of generations…"

-6-
JUST REMEMBER

Each one of us has the skills and tools to teach and deliver to children. The difference is whether we choose to use them, have the confidence to use them and know that it's okay to ask when you need help using them.

I've already explained why it's important to invest in children. As a teacher you have the opportunity to demonstrate, inspire and be a role model to the youngest of generations, equipping them in the way forward. You essentially cover three main areas as you do this:

- Encouraging them **spiritually,** to explore and form a personal relationship with Jesus.
- Encouraging them **physically,** through keeping them moving and active (a really important element for all children and their development).
- Encouraging them **emotionally,** by helping them to understand and articulate feelings through movement and dance when they may not have the capacity to speak them.

This just skims the surface of the impact that you can make, because when Jesus has the wheel, anything is possible!

Before we go further, I want to draw your attention to the story of Jesus walking on water. Take a moment to read Matthew 14:22–33.

> *Immediately Jesus made the disciples get into the boat and go on ahead of him to the other side, while he dismissed the crowd. After he had dismissed them, he went up on a mountainside by himself to pray. Later that night, he was there alone, and the boat was already a considerable distance from land, buffeted by the waves because the wind was against it.*
>
> *Shortly before dawn Jesus went out to them, walking on the lake. When the disciples saw him walking on the lake, they were terrified. "It's a ghost," they said, and cried out in fear.*

> *But Jesus immediately said to them: "Take courage! It is I. Don't be afraid."*
>
> *"Lord, if it's you," Peter replied, "tell me to come to you on the water."*
>
> *"Come," he said.*
>
> *Then Peter got down out of the boat, walked on the water and came toward Jesus. But when he saw the wind, he was afraid and, beginning to sink, cried out, "Lord, save me!"*
>
> *Immediately Jesus reached out his hand and caught him. "You of little faith," he said, "why did you doubt?"*
>
> *And when they climbed into the boat, the wind died down. Then those who were in the boat worshiped him, saying, "Truly you are the Son of God."*

What stands out to you? How could this passage be relevant when talking about equipping and releasing our youngest generation?

It's relevant because it requires a stepping out, a trust point, the ability to say, "Ok, Jesus, you've got this." Look particularly at verses 25-29.

Teaching children anything takes courage. As a teacher, there will be good days and bad days. What keeps you strong during those moments of trial? Is trusting God in your ultimate goal? Take a pause in this book now, before you get stuck into the nitty gritty. Trust that you are capable to step out and lead children. Trust that Jesus will take the wheel for you, in all circumstances. But wholeheartedly trust that God will give you every place you set your foot (Joshua 1:3).

One of the things that I cannot stress enough is to not put a limit on what children are capable of. Their maturity about certain topics or their ability to explain something better than you will always astound you. Take every opportunity to offer them the chance to step outside the boat and walk on water. They see your courage. Help them display theirs.

ACTIVITY

Part of having courage is the ability to recognise what you are struggling with, what you are afraid of and the impact it would have if you didn't do it.

For example, you could be afraid that you're not going to be able to explain things in a clear way to children, or that you won't generate enough excitement and enthusiasm with the children, or even that they won't listen to you.

What's the thing that scares you most about teaching or when teaching children?

There is nothing wrong with these fears. Remember, God is there to help you step out on the water and walk boldly on it. He is the one that can equip you!

-7-
GETTING STARTED

When we feel we just can't start something, we're often told:

"Just do *something*."

It seems pretty simple… gather a group of children at home or at church and start moving. Maybe that isn't simple for some people, so here are my best gems to help you get started.

Create a starting point for a workshop. The best places to look? The Bible and worship songs!

Start with God's word and pick something that can demonstrate movement, reflect God's character or encourage a conversation. There are so many verses you can pick from. I'm sure you have some favourite verses that offer a great starting place. But if not, try one of these:

- Exodus 15:20–21 – Miriam Dancing
- Psalm 145:8 – Slow to Anger and Rich in Love
- Matthew 6:9–13 – The Lord's Prayer
- Acts 2 – Day of Pentecost
- Luke 15:11–32 – Prodigal Son

Songs are a great starting point too. They can be descriptive about God's character, our struggles as Christians and they are good at evoking different emotions. It's useful to pick a song that the children will know, so choose one used regularly during the service or in other groups. You can use the songs to then pick themes and find Scriptures that can be woven into your workshop.

I will go into more detail about the things that I have mentioned as we progress through this book. But before we go any further, I want to encourage you that God will lead you where you need to go with the workshop and how it will progress. A tiny seed will blossom and grow into something you didn't think was possible.

Most people fall into one of two camps:

- Those that know the end result and need to work out how to get there.
- Those that need to take time with the process to see what the end result will look like.

There is no right or wrong camp. However, to progress well it's good to identify which one you are in, as this will help with your planning.

For example, let's take the song 'Over All the Earth'. Camp One will be able to visualise what the end dance or movement will look like. They will make sure that the exercises picked will enable the children to get to that point. In comparison, Camp Two won't know what the end dance, movement etc. will look like. Instead, take time to deliver exercises that prompt a response (Chapter 8 will explain this more). The response to the prompt will shape what the finished dance looks like.

Why is this important? Taking a moment to recognise how you process and piece things together will help in your planning of sessions and recognising why you pick certain things at certain points. You can be in both camps, but often there is a preference towards one.

ACTIVITY

Using the next bit of the book, I will explain my winning class structure, why it works, and how to do it effectively. I'll also discuss the key things to build confidence when working with children, using creative prayer and some workshop outlines you can use yourself.

Before then, pause and consider your answers to the following questions. The answers to them will help in your planning and understanding what's important to you when and how you plan.

What topic could you pick to get started?

Why have you chosen it?

Are you a Camp One or Camp Two planner?

-8-
WINNING WORKSHOP STRUCTURE

> *For you created my inmost being; you knit me together in my mother's womb*
> *(Psalm 139:13)*

God made us unique and individual. That is the amazing thing about how we are all made. This means how we teach and deliver will be individual as well, which is important to remember. How you interpret what I share in this book is unique to *you*.

The structure that I am going to share with you has been developed over many years of teaching, and after trying many different ways of delivery, structures and standpoints. So what I share now comes tried and tested over many years.

Some of you will have delivered a dance workshop before. This might have gone well, or it might have been a bit of a trial. You will, however, have been able to identify the key moments that you felt you had your participants' attention. Those are your nugget moments.

As you become more equipped as a teacher, you will be able to hone in on your nugget moments. Planning your sessions to allow space for you to shine during these moments will help you grow as a dance leader. The result of allowing space for these nugget moments may mean spending longer or shorter on different aspects of the workshop structure.

Let's begin to look in more detail at different aspects of the structure, why we do it and how we can implement it. The activity boxes will also contain some actions to engage you and to put into practice what you have read.

So what does the structure of a workshop look like? There are six key areas that need to be considered when planning:

- Icebreaker/warm-up
- Exploration 1
- Exploration 2
- Sequence
- Free
- Cool-down and calm

Let me reiterate: this structure is one that has worked *very* well over many years, allowing the opportunity for you to really get stuck into the workshop. However you must also note that the above elements don't always have to be in this order. I passionately believe that each one of them has a place in a workshop, but it might be that you have to alter the order.

> **ACTIVITY**
>
> Before we get going. Think about your experience as a dance leader or participant.
>
> Can you identify any nugget moments that you have had yourself or witnessed through another dance leader?
>
> Why are they memorable?

First up, the icebreaker/warm-up

This is your chance to shine and make an impression. How you start sets the tone for the rest of the workshop. Some of the following points will influence how you set out and begin your workshop.

- **Does your group know each other?** Find a fun way that everyone can introduce themselves, so participants feel more comfortable. This could be verbally or through movement.
- **Raise their heart rates.** It is important to *gradually* raise our heart rate and body temperature. This will decrease injuries and increase the body's ability to move more efficiently. You will need to make yourself aware of any existing injuries participants might have and bear in mind that, dependent on age, participants may need more 'warming up' than you may have planned.
- **Create a sense of fun.** You want to help your participants feel relaxed and safe. The warm-up is a great opportunity to let them see who you are and get moving with you.
- **Include dynamic stretches.** These are stretches that move and encourage the body to go beyond its normal range of motion, therefore stretching and moulding the muscles to work effectively. Often, we push ourselves beyond what we would normally do in a

worship dance workshop. Participants need to know their limits, but as a leader you need to ensure that you have prepared their bodies as much possible to dance the best way they can, safely.

- **Introduce the theme.** The warm-up is a fab place to subtly (or not) introduce your theme. Be creative and be literal – a game can be a great place to start. For example, take the game piggys, snakes and sharks (see resource section for more info) and adapt to three things connected to your theme.
- Finally, **have a stop signal.** This is applicable for adults and children in equal measure. Adults do love to chat and sometimes reining them in, to focus back on the task at hand, can be hard work. Similarly, children can be the same, just more excitable! I love to use "Starfish in 5, 4, 3, 2, 1." By the time I've finished counting I expect everyone to be in the shape of a starfish!

ACTIVITY
What is your biggest sparkle? What glows when you start to lead dance? If you're not leading dance yet, consider those questions in relation to any leadership you have done. You could also think about a dance leader or a leader you know and like. Can you answer these questions in relation to them?

ACTION
Create a theme-based warm-up – possible ideas could be sea/water, fire or nature. Don't forget to consider what your stop signal will be and generate a game to get the kids moving.

Exploration

The fun builds from here. During this section you should give participants tools and tricks to go deeper with the theme that you are exploring. Your aim is to enable them to *feel* a connection to the theme, as well as *explore* movement concepts attached to it. I find this is best done twice through (hence why I mention Exploration 1 and Exploration 2). The first time allows the connection and the second, the connection and exploration.

Let us take an example. You are running a session exploring stepping onto God's biblical truths. Participants have not danced or moved before with this topic. On the floor are 'stepping stones' of God's truths.

For example:
You have a purpose. (Genesis 1:27)
I love you as you are. (Jeremiah 31:3)
I know your name. (Ephesians 1:11–12)
I catch every tear. (Revelation 21:3–4)
I will carry your burdens. (2 Corinthians 1:3–4)

In the first instance, to grow the connection you want to get them moving about the stones and introduce the use of levels. A good way of doing this is via a simple exercise called 'crouch, pause, touch, engage', where touch = body part resting on body part, engage = physically connecting with a shape in some way and pause = allowing them to focus on a 'stepping stone' that they'll get to. This is Exploration 1.

To deepen the connection to the theme, you then lead participants through another exploration. In this instance, for a **second exploration,** you could discuss different ways of travelling, including how they could get between the different stones without just walking.

Taking the time to do these explorations stands the participants in better stead to feel capable and confident to go deeper in the rest of the workshop, as well as equipping them with ideas for movement.

ACTIVITY
Think of another way that you could explore the stepping stones. Consider the themes that the stepping stones are representing. How they could be demonstrated through movement or working with others.

ACTION
With connection to the theme that you picked for the warm-up earlier, decide two ways that you could explore it. What key elements do you need to include?

Sequence/development

Giving participants time to explore, whether physically or in discussions, helps to provide building blocks to enable participants to begin to build bits together that they have learnt already. So this section is all about development or creating a sequence. This might be:

- Learning a choreographed sequence using some elements from the exploration.
- Putting together their own sequence on their own, in pairs or a group based on Scriptures or other themes.
- There might even be an additional exploration needed for the purpose of your theme to enable participants to be in a good place.

The key here is that the previous explorations should have provided the springboard for this section and how you develop it.

ACTIVITY

Consider a workshop you have attended and write down how the leader brought together the sequence or development towards the end of the session.

ACTION

How could you develop the explorations you have created for your theme? Is there a sequence or development that you could teach to begin to draw it together?

Free

Having a section titled 'Free' sounds a bit random, doesn't it? But the point is that you will want something to do in between finishing the sequence and starting the cool down. Consider it a cementing or pause section based on what you have covered over the course of the workshop. The free section could be any of the following things:

- Improvised worship.
- Blessing or sharing – the chance to share with others what the participants have done throughout the workshop. What you share and what people see can be different things.
- Reflection – taking a pause to process what has been explored and what the impact has been on them and their journey of faith.

ACTIVITY
Consider the workshops you might deliver. Which one of the above 'free' ideas might fit best in your workshop structure? Why?
ACTION
Continuing the lesson plan you have been creating, how do you feel you could draw together what has been explored and created during the workshop so far?

Cool-down and calm

This is important for a couple of reasons.

1.) You have **just moved participants' bodies. Some of those participants may not be used to moving.** So it's important to demonstrate how to stretch and look after your body after you have done physical activity. Never make assumptions that participants will automatically cool down of their own accord, nor that they know what to do. It is your responsibility to not only offer the opportunity but also encourage participants to do further stretching at home, if necessary.
2.) It provides the opportunity to **draw everything together from the workshop**, pray and bless people on their journeys going forward from there, as well as ask for any feedback, if appropriate at that time.

This period of time at the end can be very special, as people share what they've learnt and how God spoke to them. With children, offering them questions to gauge their learning is really helpful. Thinking back to the theme we've looked at over the past few sections – God's stepping stones of truth – you could ask these questions:

- Which of God's truths did you love the most?
- Who can share with me their favourite movement?
- Can anyone tell me what the theme was today?

ACTIVITY
What other questions could you ask at the end of the workshop to check participants' understanding or enjoyment of the session?
ACTION
You now have the chance to finish and draw together the workshop plan that you have created. How would you do it?

Let's recap

- Begin with an icebreaker/warm-up to get people moving and introduce the theme.

- Provide opportunities to explore the theme to allow participants to feel comfortable with moving and creating.

- Draw together what they have learnt already by either creating a choreographed sequence or giving space for participants to create something themselves.

- Open the space to share and bless others or worship individually.

- Finish by drawing everyone back together, stretching and focusing on what people have discovered.

ACTIVITY

You have a workshop plan!!! Give yourself a pat on the back. This is just the beginning. As I've shared, there are many ways you can create themes for workshops.

Think about one of your favourite Bible verses. How could you develop a workshop based on that?

-9-
CONFIDENCE IN LEADING CHILDREN

Working with children can bring so many delightful moments, as well as stressful moments. Having clear boundaries and knowing how you will teach and deal with issues as they arise will help you deliver a more effective session. Here are some tips to consider.

Know the area you are working in

This is where you are creating a safe space, so the size and how many children it can hold are really key. You need an awareness of whether there are any nooks and crannies they could escape and hide in (it does happen!), as well as where the toilets are and how many leaders you would ideally have to assist or lead with you.

Give clear, precise commands

Children respond best when they know where the boundaries are. This includes giving them set timeframes to complete their work in. For example, you want them to create two movements: one that shows when they are happy and one when they are sad. So you can say to them, 'You have until the count of 10 to make your happy position… 10, 9, 8, 7…' You then repeat with a position for sad. I would recommend repeating the happy and then sad position again in order to cement the children's movement memory.

'Lock it away'

This is a phrase I use (even with adults!) when I have either taught something or the children have just made something up and we are moving onto something else, but you want to encourage them to remember what they've just done. We pretend to take a key and lock the side of our head. That physical action helps the children recognise they will need to recall what they have just learnt.

Engage

Your workshop won't be effective if you can't engage with the children. Try using **eye contact** and **crouching down** to their level if they are shorter than you. Make things fun. Use imagery and association to help keep their attention.

Safety

The children's safety, but also your own, is very important. Whoever you are delivering a workshop for or on behalf of, it is essential that you have the following in place as a minimum: risk assessment, DBS (Disclosure and Barring Service) checks, best working practices for children, child protection policy, workshop guidelines and first aid kit.

Effective ways of delivery

Demonstrate, demonstrate, demonstrate – the one key word!

Demonstrating is so important for the visual learners in your group to understand the task more clearly. For the self-conscious, shy and unsure, they can copy, hide and gain inspiration through watching you move. Don't be shy to demonstrate and dance!

I will just take a moment here to talk about ways of learning. Generally speaking, there are three ways of learning: audio, visual and kinaesthetic. Each of us tends to have a preference towards one. Within your delivery and planning this is important to remember. How you learn will be different to others. Audio learners love to hear how you describe and speak about the exercise. Visual learners want to see you move and demonstrate it, whilst kinaesthetic learners want to keep doing it themselves, over and over.

The following four techniques will help you deliver to different learners:

1. Mirroring

Teaching children movement is best done via mirroring the movement when facing them. This enables them to always see the movements you are doing clearly. It also allows you to see the children and whether you have their focus – or whether they're misbehaving! The tricky thing about mirroring is learning to teach everything in the opposite direction. Naturally we teach with the right side leading, but when you mirror, you teach with the left side leading. It's a bit hard to get the hang of, but when you do, it's invaluable. If you have more than one dance leader or an assistant, one can be amongst the children facing the front with them. Then the leader faces the children.

2. Chunking

This is a very technical term you will find in many books… or perhaps just mine! I find it the best way to describe how to divide the material you're teaching into manageable chunks. If you tried to learn everything at once, you would struggle. So, as with anything, it's best broken down. For a dance workshop, this looks like – teach a little, practise and reinforce it, then teach a little more. Every time you teach a little more, when you reinforce or recap it, do it from the starting point.

3. Association/imagery

Children will associate and remember movements much more easily if they know something that they can remember alongside it. For example, stand tall like a soldier, be small like a ball, be floppy like a puppet, draw a big sun in the sky etc.

4. Dance with them

Always take the time to dance with the children, and always dance it to the best of your ability. They'll be inspired!

Working with varying levels and abilities

This can be the most daunting of tasks when working with children – the unknown of how quick a group or individuals may learn, interact or react to the workshop material. My biggest tip here is to not rush, to take a pause and a deep breath. Then, in your preparation, try to add at least one other way (two is even better) of completing a task.

For example, you ask every child to create three movements based on the emotion of love. An easier version of this is that they create a still or a 'freeze' of between one and three movements. A harder version is that they create three movements and link them together one after the other. An in-between version would be creating three movements and getting used to moving between each movement, doing them one after the other. Think back to where I described the exploration section in Chapter 8. The above all work really well as explorations adapted for each specific theme you teach.

A good way to think about it is high, medium or low tasks. Generally, you would deliver a workshop to medium level. You make a presumption that some things are already there, and there's the option to expand if needed. Everyone (not just children) has room for growth. As a teacher and leader, it is your job to encourage, nurture and develop that growth. That means identifying those that might be struggling and therefore need a 'lower' task, as well as those that want to explore more and need a 'higher' task.

It should be noted that you shouldn't single people out because of their abilities. Instead, if you know there are a few that would benefit from an alternative option, create a group for that option and then a group for another option. Or have everyone build up from the lower option. Everyone grows and starts from the same starting point.

ACTIVITY

Creating your own way of working takes time. Allow yourself to realise what's important to you as you teach, share and deliver.

What guidelines or principles could you lay out for children's workshops to create a safe space, enhance the experience and give clear understanding to all?

-10-
CREATIVE PRAYER, CHILDREN AND DANCING

This is something that I was drawn to as I taught more and my work with UC Grace developed. Children, just like adults, respond to and interact differently to learning. After all, God did make us unique! It made sense to me that the interaction of prayer during sessions was really important and providing ways for different ages to engage in this is something I became passionate about.

I've always been passionate about being creative in what I deliver and how I choose to engage with those I teach. For me, that's an essential quality of UC Grace – a quality that God has encouraged me in and an aspect that challenges me to share more of God in an alternative way. But drawing this into children's workshops can be challenging, and I hope to share some ways that I have achieved that.

What is creative prayer?

This can be very personal. Just like creativity is an individual thing, so too is creative prayer. I define it as praying and responding to Scripture outside the box, providing an opportunity to deepen a conversation with God through different artistic outlets. This can include, but is not limited to, art and craft, dancing, speaking, singing and writing. There is no limit to the ways you choose to connect to God and His word.

With children, I have found that adding in layers of creative prayer during sessions helps them to process, cement and determine for themselves the theme or aspect of faith that we are exploring. Here are just some ways that I have used creative prayer:

Topic: Jonah and the Whale | Fishing Net Prayer

Age group: 3–8 years

Activity: take a piece of wool or ribbon and tie it on or weave it into the net.

Discussion or learning: encourage discussion about following Jesus and listening to him. Pray for God's blessing and confidence to follow Jesus.

Topic: Noah's Ark | You Are You

Age group: 2–5 years

Activity: make a small rainbow out of the children's fingerprints.

Discussion or learning: this encourages children to identify that there is only one of them. Their finger is unique to just them. It will allow conversations of how they are different from their friends.

Topic: Advent | Prayer Bunting (can fit with many themes)

Age group: all ages

Activity: to make the bunting, you will need different pieces of cream coloured material – rectangular shapes work well – and various craft bits to decorate them. Think of things you are thankful for, enjoy and can see in God. Decorate the shapes however you want, to reflect what you think of. Choose a ribbon to string the pieces together and hang it up as a reminder.

Discussion or learning: have a conversation with God as you make it! For younger ones, parents can have a general conversation with them about things that they enjoy and talk about how God made it, designed it and helps us with it.

But how can that link in with dance?

Many activities used for creative prayer are also prompts to create movement. We have discussed how creative prayer or movement is about thinking creatively and challenging the way we might normally address a theme or piece of Scripture. Different activities will speak to different children depending on their unique tools and understanding.

For example, with Jonah and the Whale this can linked to movement by exploring:

- Follow-the-leader-type games and exercises.
- Moving with others as one.
- Exploring listening to God through taking it in turns to do a movement between partners.
- Talking about confidence and how we can have confidence as we walk.

Whether you choose to include a form of creative prayer during your workshop is up to you. However, I would encourage you to at least explore it individually and see where it takes you!

> **ACTIVITY**
>
> As I dipped my toe further and further into creative prayer, I found it blurred the edges of using movement in prayer. For older children and young people, this transition and concept of moving prayers or prayer dance may be integral to them developing their faith. For those that don't have the confidence to speak prayers out loud, having the space to pray creatively or through movement can open up so many possibilities.
>
> Design a creative prayer activity along one of the following themes: Light in Darkness, Our Father, The Lost Sheep, Creation.

Jesus *for* Kids: Teaching *Dance* and Sharing *Faith*

Part Four
Moving Forward

"You can only understand the limitations of your teaching when you constantly expose yourself to the situations where your skills can be challenged."

-11-
READY-TO-GO WORKSHOPS

The best way to develop your skills as a children's dance leader is practise, practise, practise, and with children! You can only understand the limitations of your teaching when you constantly expose yourself to the situations where your skills can be challenged. Delivering a whole workshop may seem too much right away. That's why it's important to do it in stages. Work with someone else that you can split things between, and take it in turns to deliver different bits. This will allow you to identify areas that you need to grow, have more confidence in or seek clarity over.

Remember, you can do this. God has built in you the ability for you to do it. If you've taken the time to identify why you are dancing and why you are using your faith and dance to share with children, God will reveal to you the path you need to go on and give you all the tools that are needed for you to do it.

This section contains some ready-to-go workshops. I have also built a glossary of terms and a list of resources at the back of this book. You can refer to them as you read through the workshop plans in this section.

These plans are meant to act as a guide and shouldn't be used word for word. Why? You are an individual and you will teach with a different emphasis to me. Therefore, you need to make them your own. Own them and put your stamp on them. Let them ignite your confidence and draw you to a place of exploration. Most of all, let them act as a springboard to create even more amazing workshops than what I have written.

JONAH AND THE WHALE

Aim: to recognise that God talks to us and we can choose how we listen and respond.

Age group: 3–8 years

Icebreaker/warm-up

Follow-my-leader to form a circle in the centre of the room or dance space.

Hello song[3] and names.

Warm-up – using the song 'Great Big God', work your way through the actions. On the instrumental break in the song, march into the centre of the circle and then out. Practise getting tall, small and wide.

Musical Statues – stay in a circle and form a different shape each time the music stops. Have children explore the tempo of the music between freezes – marching fast and slow, and making themselves tall, small and wide.

Exploration 1 – exploring their body and creating movements.

Staying in a circle, using two balls (one large, one small), throw/roll/catch the balls across the circle. Encourage the children to think about how they move. When they throw, roll or catch the balls, ask them to consider different levels, like tall, small and wide and creating contact with the floor and other children.

Then remove the balls and pretend you're all holding a ball. Expand your hands to hold a big one, make it small, move around with it. What different ways could the children explore movement with their imaginary ball?

Exploration 2 – the story

(Before the workshop, hide some pictures of ships and whales.)

---

[3] The 'Hello song' is much like a welcome song. Make up your own version!

JONAH AND THE WHALE (continued)

Play follow-my-leader to collect the ships and whales hidden round the room.

Talk about different ways God could talk to us.

Introduce the story – interactively.

(You could gather a boat, Lego man, small house and felt or blue fabric for the sea. Use these as you tell the story. If you also hide enough ships and whales for a child to have one each, these can be incorporated too.)

> *There was a man named Jonah. Jonah told people messages from God. One day God told Jonah to go to Nineveh and tell the people there that they had been bad and their city was to be destroyed. Instead Jonah ran away and got on a boat. God sent a strong wind. The wind came and the waves came. The sailors were scared. Jonah was sleeping and was asked to pray. But Jonah said the storm had come because of him. So he was thrown overboard and a large fish swallowed him. He was inside the fish for three days and three nights whilst he prayed to God. God told the large fish to throw Jonah out. Jonah did what God had asked him to do and went to Nineveh. The people were very sorry and started to listen to God. Yay!*

God has an important message to tell us all and we need to listen to hear it. (Story based on Scripture from Jonah 1–4.)

Standing in a space, ask the children to be as quiet as they can be – what can they hear? Help them by suggesting some things that are heard in the room during the silence. Did they need to listen hard to hear them?

To encourage movement, ask a question and explore with movement:

Who knows how the wind moves? Let's explore being the wind.

JONAH AND THE WHALE (continued)

What about the waves, how do they move? Are they big or small, strong or gentle?

Explore jumping, thinking about being thrown overboard and thrown out of the large fish.

Sequence

Teach a dance using ribbons. For example, walk round in a circle, holding the ribbons high above your head. Draw a rainbow with the ribbons by starting your rainbow outside the circle and taking them up and into the middle. Continue taking the ribbons down. Spin round on the spot, with your ribbons trailing along the floor. Flick your ribbons into the centre, and out. Wave your ribbons up high.

Praise time/free dancing

Pop on some music for the children to worship and move to, however they feel led. Join in with them, so they can see you worship too.

Cool-down/calm

Whale prayers – gather around a net/blue material and talk about how God hears us and we should listen to Him. Have a quiet moment, waiting.

Cool-down – ask children to sit or lie down and using a large piece of fabric, waft it up and down over everyone (you could use the song 'Come and Make My Heart Your Home', Powerpack Children's Ministries).

To finish – read a story, sing the song 'Twinkle Twinkle' with actions if you want and a goodbye song.

GO, GO, GO JOSEPH

Aim: a fun way of recognising how we can trust God and learning a fun dance to the song 'Go, Go, Go Joseph'.

Age group: 5–11 years

Warm-up

Moving around the space, call out the following actions for the children to do and then move on:

- Jump
- Slide
- Spin
- Stretch
- Balance
- Find a group of... (call out a certain number for them to get into groups of)

Exploration 1 – trust, catch and fall

Safety point: you will know the children you are working with and also how much assistance you have. It is your responsibility to risk assess the appropriateness of this exercise and adapt the number of children that may do it at once if necessary.

Split the children into pairs and demonstrate ways they can explore catch and fall with trust, by falling forwards, sideways and backwards. Here are some key points to remember:

(A is the 'catcher' and B is the 'faller'.)

- A needs to have one foot in front of the other with their legs planted down in a lunge. They need to keep their back straight and use the transfer of weight from their front foot to their back foot to 'absorb' the weight of B when they catch them.
- A will need to communicate when B should fall with a countdown.

GO, GO, GO JOSEPH (continued)

- A's palms should be open and facing towards B.
- With all the falls, start close and then gradually move further away. A should use the bend in their knees to catch and absorb the person falling, transferring their weight to take them deeper into the fall when needed.

Backwards fall – B needs to ensure that they stay completely straight. Imagine there is a pole down their back. Keep their shoulders down, no tension in their neck and hands crossed on their chest.

Sideways fall – A stands to the side of B, with their chest facing the outside of B's shoulder. B has their feet shoulder-width apart with a slight bend. B must keep their back straight as they fall sideways.

Forwards fall – A will catch B by the shoulders. B must really remember not to wiggle at the waist but to stay straight.

Exploration 2 – movements and steps

Teach these different moves for the children to explore to some music:

- Side hop with arm wiggle
- Double arm punch, high then low
- Side lift
- Flag work – holding it safely, figure of 8s, rainbows, turning

Sequence

This short sequence was created to the song 'Go, Go, Go Joseph' from the musical *Joseph and the Amazing Technicolour Dreamcoat* soundtrack. The children learnt a set of movements together and were then split into groups (some with flags, some without flags) and learnt different movements. You have the option to split the children up further into smaller groups afterwards to choreograph something on their own if you wish.

GO, GO, GO JOSEPH (continued)

Everyone needs to learn this:
- 16 counts moving into a space
- 4 counts wiggle on the spot
- 4 x double arm punch – high then low
- Link arm with partner, spin round and repeat in the other direction
- Side lift first person, side lift second person
- Half split off to get flags

If children have flags:

8 counts march back into space
4 counts turning, 4 counts circle flag above
4 counts walk F, swing flag behind
4 counts walk B, swing flag forwards

Repeat.
Hand flag to partner
Shimmy and look – tilting top half of body, going alternate ways ↔
March F x 8, B x 8 – figure of 8s
Rainbow R/L x 2

If they don't have flags:

Shimmy F/B x 2
Claps F/H/R/L (16 in total)
Shimmy and look tilting top half of body, going alternate ways ↔
Crouch down low

Free

Have some fun time practising with a flag and doing the dance. Give the children the opportunity to share what they have created and learnt with others.

Cool-down and calm

Take time to stretch out your arms after the flag work. Everyone lies down on the floor, taking a moment to think about trusting God and what bits of their life they need to trust Him more with.

FAMILY ADVENT FUN

Aim: recognise the joy we can get from movement and dance and put some movement to a prayer.

Age group: family, all ages

Welcome song and movement

Advent is a time of hope and waiting for Jesus. We'll start by reading some of God's word and praying – Romans 15:12–15

> And again, Isaiah says, "The Root of Jesse will spring up, one who will arise to rule over the nations; in him the Gentiles will hope." May the God of hope fill you with all joy and peace as you trust in him, so that you may overflow with hope by the power of the Holy Spirit.
>
> I myself am convinced, my brothers and sisters, that you yourselves are full of goodness, filled with knowledge and competent to instruct one another. Yet I have written you quite boldly on some points to remind you of them again, because of the grace God gave me

Warm-up – wiggle song; tall, small and wide; different shapes.

Learn first part of the dance

Dance – 'It's a New Day' | 'Awesome Cutlery' (available on music apps and YouTube)

Thank you, Father, for today | Reach right arm, then left, up, upwards and pull down, arms at right angles

Teach me how to choose your way | Parallel arms forward

Help me lift my eyes to see, who you are | Open arms out wide and then take arms high

FAMILY ADVENT FUN (continued)

You are faithful, always true | Place the right palm onto left palm on left side, then left on right side
Every good thing comes from you | Push hands away bouncing them and your knees
Meet me in your word and help me worship you | Book sign, jump clap, jump clap
It's a new, new day, to sing your praise | Arms to V and pull down, praise hands
It's a new, new day, to walk in your ways | Arms to V and pull down, march on the spot
It's a new, new day, to make you known | Arms to V and pull down, hands to temple
It's a new, new day to see your kingdom grow | Arms to V and pull down, make big circle

Exploration – movement to own prayers – family choreography opportunity

Identify four words that you can build movement from to make a prayer:

Thank God for…
Need help with…
Say sorry for…
Dream about…

With younger children, approach this really simply and relate it to what they know.

Learn next bit of dance

Jesus you are all I need | Spin round, arms out

Thank you that you died for me | Thank-you sign, make a cross

Help me know you'll always be | (In partners) slap right hand, slap left hand, hit right hand and spin around

FAMILY ADVENT FUN (continued)

Here with me | Hands onto chest

I am weak, but you are strong | Drop down, then come up and do strong arms

When I stumble you hold on | Hold hands with people around you

Help me turn away from sin and worship you | Step back same foot and arm. Drawing arm away from front. Turn back to front and bow down.

Exploration – free dance and movement opportunity

Have a quick talk about movement with ribbons and how you should remember that when you pick up a ribbon you are using it to worship God. Ribbons are a significant sign of battle and putting a stake in the ground to talk to God, worship and pray.

Allow space for exploration with ribbons and time to worship.

Full dance

To draw the dance together, you can add in the family choreography that was created around prayers to the section below:

It's a gift of time you give,
One more day for us to live,
One more chance for us to call
On the name of Christ the Lord

Cool-down

Find a space and lie down on the ground, if able. Whilst the participants take a pause at the end, read Romans 15:12–15 to them slowly. Talk through some stretches for them to do too.

THE LORD IS MY SHEPHERD

Aim: to understand the shepherd stays with their sheep. We are sheep and God is the shepherd.

Age group: under 5 years

Warm-up

Welcome song. Play 'wiggle, wiggle, wiggle, freeze' to some music. Copy and response – you do a move and they copy. Read through Psalm 23.

Exploration 1

Ask the children what words they can hear in the psalm. Pick out words that they can understand and encourage the children to describe what they mean. Possible words could include shepherd, green pastures, quiet waters, guide, fear, overflow. Can the children think of and try making any movements to the words? Keep a dialogue going and demonstrate different movements.

Exploration 2

Say to the children, "God is like a shepherd that cares for us. A sheep follows his shepherd. Let's play a game called 'follow the shepherd'." Lead the children around the space, exploring height, width and size with movements.

Dance

Working with the children, help them to identify movements that they liked from Exploration 1 and actions that you did from Exploration 2. Due to their age, you will need to recap the movements from each of the explorations, which will involve demonstrating. Pick three or four that you could link together for them into a short sequence.

THE LORD IS MY SHEPHERD (continued)

Free worship

Allow the children time just to dance and move, but then encourage a 'leader' that everyone has to copy. Take it in turns so all the children have a go.

Cool-down

Take the children down to the floor to stretch out. Ask questions about what you have explored during the session.

THE FAITH OF A MUSTARD SEED

Aim: realising small things can have a big impact!

Age group: 8–11 years

Begin the workshop by talking about mustard seeds. How they are one of the smallest seeds that can grow into one of the largest plants – birds can perch and build nests in them!

The kingdom of God grew from a handful of disciples. Each time we tell someone about Jesus, the kingdom grows.

Read Matthew 13:31–32 and then pray.

Warm-up

Get the children moving around the space, exploring tall, small and wide movements. Ask them how they can grow from small to big and explore different ways they could do this. Does copying someone help or hinder?

Exploration 1

Divide the children down into smaller groups of about five. Can they explore different ways of connecting as a chain? Can the chain move as one? What helps or hinders it?

Exploration 2 – cross the space

Still working in their smaller groups, direct the children to move across from one side of the room to the other, each person in the team moving one at a time. Can they do it individually or do they all need each other?

Dance

Draw together the different ways they have been moving and

THE FAITH OF A MUSTARD SEED (continued)

exploring during the session. Growing and expanding from the warm-up, supporting each other to grow and move across the space, creating a chain. Build everyone's contributions into a short sequence.

Consider using a large piece of material that you and your assistant hold up for the children to go underneath. Lower the fabric down and ask the children to grow. As they 'grow', raise and move the fabric.

Cool-down

Ask the children to become still, close their eyes and listen to a prayer from you that encourages them to listen in to God and trust that what God has planted in them will grow. Finish with some stretches and questions to check they understand what they have covered.

Where imagination and movement have no limit...

Glossary of Terms

This list contains some of the words and phrases used within the ready-to-go workshops. It's worth looking at the UC Grace YouTube channel (www.youtube.com/user/ucgracedirector), as many of the specific movements are available to watch as a video on there.

B – Back

Balance – An even distribution of weight that enables a person to remain steady in their pose.

Double arm punch, high then low – Have your feet in parallel and knees slightly bent. Raise both arms above the head in parallel and punch twice into the air, then lower and punch once downwards.

F – Forwards

Jump – Push oneself off a surface and into the air by using the muscles in one's legs and feet.

L – Left

Lunge – Placing one foot forward with knee bent at right angles and foot flat to ground. The other foot is positioned behind, knee bent at right angles and the heel raised.

Praise hands – Barrel roll hands over each other, a bit like you're winding something up and raise your hands up to the sky as you do it.

R – Right

Reach – Stretch out a body part in order to touch or grasp something.

Shimmy F/B – Place one foot forward and one foot back. Wiggle hips and shoulders forward, transfer weight onto front foot, taking a bend in the knees. Then wiggle hips and shoulders backwards transferring weight back at the same time.

Side hop with arm wiggle – A hop is a slight or small jump. For a side hop, this is done onto a single foot. Jump onto a single foot to the side.

As you do that, take your arm straight up and then draw it downwards, wiggling it.

Side lift – With a partner, lifting them up sideways. See below for breakdown. Video available on the UC Grace YouTube channel.

> Prep – A lifts and B is lifted. A positions themself side on to B, feet shoulder-width apart. B stands beside A with their inside hips close to each other. B's inside arm goes round A's neck and A takes hold of B's hand with their outside hand. A reaches around B and places their inside hand on B's outside hip. B places their hand on top. B should have a slight bend on their inside leg.

> Lift – Transfer of weight is the biggest thing to grasp to complete this lift and aiming to keep the inside hips connected. Transfer weight towards the side that B is on. Bend the knees. Keeping the bend, transfer weight back the other way. As you transfer the weight back, A needs to push B's inside hip away with their inside hip. This will cause B's outside leg to go into the air and their inside leg to come up off the ground. Transfer weight back towards B as they land.

Slide – Move smoothly along a surface whilst maintaining continuous contact with it.

Spin – Turn or whirl around quickly.

Stretch – Straighten or extend a specific body part.

Transfer of weight – Moving support from one foot to the other one, fully or partially.

Wiggle – Moving hips and shoulders side to side. Often your body naturally isolates body parts as you do this and you will be transferring your weight from side to side at the same time.

Resources

There are so many things that can support you in your journey into teaching children about faith and dance. Here are just a few things that have been useful along my journey.

Props

- Short ribbons
- Small flags
- Small and big organza juggling scarves
- Large piece of fabric
- Floor shapes or spots to stand on
- Stickers for names
- Paper, pens and crayons for any writing or drawing
- Suggested resources – hide pictures of ships and whales around the room, have a net or large piece of material, ribbons/scarves

Music

- Rend Co Kids
- God is Bigger
- Great Big God
- So Many Ways to Praise the Lord
- We Want More
- This is Awesome Cutlery
- Chuffed – Doug Horley
- Newsongs for kids – God Suit On
- You Won't Let Go
- Shine
- Lion and the Lamb
- Good, Good Father
- Come and Make My Heart Your Home
- Twinkle Twinkle
- Go, Go, Go Joseph from the musical *Joseph and the Amazing Technicolour Dreamcoat*

Links

www.ucgrace.co.uk
www.youtube.com/ucgracedirector
www.ucgrace.co.uk/Blog
www.powerpackministries.co.uk
www.guildfordbaptist.org
www.jubilee.church

www.cdfb.org.uk
www.icdf.com
www.awesomecutlery.com

Other Movement Ideas – Games and Action Songs

Please find below a selection of games and actions songs that you can use when teaching children. Some I mention in the book; others I hope provide inspiration for your planning!

The idea with most of them is that they can also transfer into some kind of warm-up and offer you ideas of how you could adapt your themes into games.

There is the assumption that most involve the children moving around the space or within a given area, either walking fast/running depending upon which instruction you have given them; once they have done the action/movement that is needed, they resume their moving. Also, to add a bit of a competition element to it, you could start eliminating the young person who completes the movement/action last.

Twinkle, twinkle

Use flashing hands when talking about the twinkles. Reach up high and then make a world sign by drawing a big circle with your arms, followed by a diamond sign with your fingers. Finish with more flashing hands.

You can listen on this link: https://youtu.be/yCjJyiqpAuU.

Wiggle, wiggle, wiggle, freeze (also known as the 'Wiggle Song', by Little Angels, New Wine)

Following the words in the song, children respond with the right movement. You can listen to the 'Wiggle Song' via this link: https://youtu.be/f5NSRdf4zYA.

Crouch, pause, touch, engage

Where crouch = making themselves small, touch = body part resting on body part, engage = physically connecting with a shape in some way, and pause = encourages them to stop and focus.

Follow my leader

Using the whole movement area you have, line the children up behind you and have them follow you and the movements you create around the room. Once you have done it for a bit, step out and to the back. The child at the front now becomes the leader, and the children and you have to copy their movements. Continue the process, giving as many children (that want to) a go.

Great big God

There are a few variations on the actions to this song. But if you check out this link, you can see one version with the lyrics: https://www.youtube.com/watch?v=xIqEDBPlBVo.

Tall, small, wide

This game encourages children to explore different sizes and the space around them. Tall means explore height, small means explore size, and wide means explore shape.

Name and action

This works best with the group size being no more than ten and when you know you are going to be seeing the people periodically across a day or regularly in the future.

- It's as the name suggests – you go round the circle and as the young person says their name, they put an action to it, preferably a big and expressive one.
- For example, I would go "My name is Anna" and at the same time do a big jump in the air, reaching as high as I could.
- Everyone would then copy. Once everyone has had a go and done their action, the idea is then to go round the circle, doing everyone's names and actions continually, gradually getting faster.

Note: depending how big and expressive the children's moves are, you can use this as part of a warm-up.

Traffic lights

This is as the name suggests: red = stop, green = go, amber = an additional movement/ transition movement of your choice.

- Then, add some fun by introducing different colours in: blue, yellow, purple etc., each one signalling a different way of travelling – run, hop, skip, jump, forwards/backwards, slow/fast.
- Use yours and their imaginations.
- You can also use it as a game, where the person who does the movement last is out.

Numbers

This runs along the same lines as traffic lights, except these are movements on the spot, as opposed to travelling ones.

- For example, one could be to jump in the air, touch the floor and walk off again; two, turn on the spot; three, find a partner, hold hands, then (both) facing each other, lean out with all your weight, lower to floor without breaking hold and then stand up again; and four could be sit down on the floor and stand up again.
- Also try it with the numbers signalling the size of groups they need to get into.
- All the time between movements, the young people should constantly be moving around the space.

Piggys, snakes and sharks

This one is just a bit of fun!

Piggys = piggyback

Snakes = lie on your belly on the floor and wriggle along

Sharks = lie on your back with your feet in the air

Play some music, and each time the music stops, call out one of the words.

About the Author

Anna Gilderson is a dancer, teacher, choreographer and writer. Her passion is to teach and share about the interaction between dance and movement and how that exploration helps us to have a deeper conversation with God.

Anna is mum to two crazy children and wife to an RAF crewman, which means a lot of the time she's juggling business, family and military deployments. But the wealth of knowledge she has learnt through leaning on God during those times has made her stronger.

Dance and movement have always been a part of her life. The journey it has allowed her to go on has enabled her to grow stronger in her faith, relationships, business and as a person. Over 10 years ago she started UC Grace, over a simple desire to just share what God gave her. As she began that journey, she learnt a lot about how God speaks to her, how God uses her to speak to others and how when you truly let the Holy Spirit step in to lead a workshop, it always makes you go wow!

Putting time in for other passions is integral to how she leads life. Sewing for pleasure, making clothes and sewing to create dancing resources such as flags, streamers and ribbons. Reading books about prayer, faith and everyday living. Putting pen to paper and starting to write for herself. Putting together resource books and training manuals to help others. Creating dance and movement prayer devotionals and numerous blog posts to encourage others in the journey of faith – whether that's through movement or not.

Her ultimate passion is sharing how you can deepen your faith through movement and dance. For her, the connection of faith and dance is synonymous in the way that she lives life. Whether people realise it or not, the relationship between movement and faith exists in everyone's everyday. Opening our Bible to read, bowing our head in prayer, raising our hand in worship, kneeling to take a pause to remember – they are all movements ingrained in you without knowing. Anna's heart is to help others recognise that those movements can create a deeper relationship with God.

In essence, she loves encouraging, growing and releasing others to their full potential, using dance and movement. Dance has always featured in some way in Anna's life and it is her go-to to connect with God and draw closer to him. If she's offered the chance to introduce others to this possibility, she jumps with both feet into the deep puddle and lets God lead!

About UC Grace

UC Grace is a dance company passionate about sharing ways of putting Jesus front and centre in life and generating deeper conversations with God, which together enable people to find grace in their everyday life. This is done by:

- Encouraging creativity and movement in people's conversations with God.
- Growing people's movement and faith to deepen their conversations with God.
- Releasing people to share how their movement can impact on their faith.

UC Grace runs dance mornings, trainings and dance weekends for all levels of ability. It also provides both practical and written resources to help people to go deeper with God and develop their leadership skills.

These values encase what we do and why we do it. Each value helps us walk with you, your faith and your dance, on your journey.

The Christian faith –

Underpins all that we do, putting Jesus front and centre. Sharing inspiring Bible verses, passages and blog posts that generate conversations.

Encouragement –

Taking the time to encourage each person in who they are, providing training and advice, a listening ear and empathy.

Creativity –

A passion to pass on our knowledge, skills and mindset by going outside the box, through various events, and training and challenging the use of resources across the arts.

Development –

Providing opportunities to develop dance techniques, interaction of movement, faith foundation and skills, by supporting, praying and growing people.

Sharing –

Dance, faith, prayer and movement is fun! We LOVE sharing and creating memories through teaching, videos, blog posts and more. Allowing movement to bless others and be blessed through movement ourselves.

If you'd like to explore more, take a look at the UC Grace blog. There is lots of information that allows you to develop what you are passionate about.

www.ucgrace.co.uk/Blog

UC Grace regularly runs both online and in-person training and development days. If you'd like us to work alongside you to develop something, then please get in touch.

We would love to know how this book has impacted your journey of dance, dance life and teaching skills. So please do get in touch and let us know.

www.ucgrace.co.uk

Facebook: @ucgracedance

Instagram: @uc.grace

www.ingramcontent.com/pod-product-compliance
Lightning Source LLC
Chambersburg PA
CBHW070925080526
44589CB00013B/1430